Goodnight OLE MISS®

Written by Courtney Solon Brown and Andrea Lea
Illustrated by Matt Gardner

AMP&RSAND, INC.

Chicago • New Orleans

Goodnight Ole Miss is part of the Goodnight Team Series
and is published in cooperation with Morgan McDaniel, LLC.
www.goodnightteam.com

ISBN 978-1467545259

Design: David Robson, Robson Design

Published by
AMPERSAND, INC.
1050 North State Street
Chicago, Illinois 60610

---

203 Finland Place
New Orleans, Louisiana 70131

---

www.ampersandworks.com

Produced and Published in the United States

January 2014
Printed by WeSP, Gyeonggi-do, Korea
WESP-JT-130415-R1

1st Edition

The authors wish to thank the following who allowed use of their images for reference: Cliff Holley,
Mary Elizabeth Milek Sessums, Roy M. Sessums, Angie Wells, and Phillip Waller, phillipwaller.com.

And a very special thank you to Lynn C. Woo for the many reference photos she provided.

**To request a personalized copy
or to schedule a book signing/school reading, email
goodnightolemiss@gmail.com**

For Kai, Jane Clare

and little Rebels everywhere

There is a university with a beauty so great

Nestled among the kudzu hills of the Magnolia State

Red and blue are school colors so bold

The Pride of the South plays songs of old

Traditions, historic buildings, and true Southern grace

Are what make Ole Miss® a welcoming place

After heading to bed and saying goodnight

Let dreams of becoming a Rebel take flight

Goodnight Red, Goodnight Blue

Goodnight students writing papers that are due

Goodnight to The Grove™ with trees so tall

Goodnight Vaught-Hemingway and the boys of fall

Goodnight Walk of Champions, fans smell victory in the air

Goodnight Grove tailgaters with food and drink to share

Goodnight Lyceum, on The Circle it stands

Goodnight Tad Pad™ and cheering basketball fans

Goodnight to The Square and its courthouse so white

Goodnight grand houses bathed in early evening light

Goodnight Ventress Hall with spires so high

Goodnight Civil Rights Monument lit against the night sky

Goodnight Double Decker Festival, celebrating art in the spring

Goodnight Paris-Yates Chapel™ and the peace you bring

Goodnight Rowan Oak with writing on the wall

Goodnight Swayze Field™ where umps cry, "PLAY BALL!"

Goodnight 18, it's the speed we drive

Goodnight to our memories that seem so alive

Goodnight Ole Miss® with your history so deep

Hotty Toddy™ Rebels™! It's time to sleep.

OLE MISS-OLOGY

University of Mississippi,® nicknamed Ole Miss,® is a public university located in Oxford, Mississippi. The school first held classes in 1848 for 80 entering students, and it was the only public university in Mississippi for the next 23 years. The official school colors, adopted in 1893, are the crimson (red) of Harvard and the blue of Yale.

Civil Rights Monument Dedicated in 2006, the monument commemorates the efforts of James Meredith, the first black student enrolled at the university in 1962 during the civil rights movement, and others who fought for equal education opportunities in the South.

Double Decker Arts Festival First held in 1995, this festival celebrating art, music and food is enjoyed every spring on and around the Square in Oxford.

18 mph Speed Limit In honor of the jersey number worn by Archie Manning, a former starting quarterback for the football team, the speed limit on campus is set at 18 miles per hour.

The Grove™ Approximately 10 acres of beautiful green space located centrally on campus, this is where much of the legendary tailgating of Ole Miss takes place. Since 1990, vehicles have been prohibited in the Grove, and so, on game day, a sea of red, blue and white tents stretch as far as the eye can see. Under these tents, finely-dressed tailgaters celebrate by the light of candelabras with elaborate food spreads served on silver platters. True Southern hospitality is on display as tailgaters invite and welcome strangers to partake in their celebrations.

Hotty Toddy™ is used as both a greeting and a cheer among Ole Miss Rebel fans. When you hear "Are you READY?" yelled on game days, you know the cheer of "Hotty Toddy" is about to begin.

Are you READY?
Heck yes, darn right!

Hotty Toddy, Gosh almighty
Who are we? Hey!
Flim Flam, Bim Bam
Ole Miss, Yes Ma'am!

The Lyceum™ The oldest building on campus, it was completed in 1848, although the north and south wings weren't added until 1903. During the Civil War, the Lyceum was used as a hospital for both Union and Confederate soldiers, and horses carried carts of the wounded right through the large double front doors. Some 700 soldiers who died at the university hospital were buried in a cemetery on the grounds of the university. Today, the Lyceum houses the administrative offices of the university.

Paris-Yates Chapel™ The interfaith chapel on campus is a place for prayer, meditation and worship. The funds for the chapel all came from private donations, including ones from the namesake families. The Peddle Bell Tower, a gift from the Peddle family, features 36 bronze bells, which ring every hour and half-hour, and every day at 5 p.m., the bells play a group of songs.

The Pride of the South is the nickname for the University of Mississippi marching band, first organized in 1928.

Ole Miss

Rebel, the Black Bear The official sporting mascot of Ole Miss, named in 2010. Two types of black bears are found in Mississippi, and the teddy bear, a widely popular toy, came about because of a hunting trip taken by President Theodore "Teddy" Roosevelt in Mississippi in 1902. Roosevelt had been invited by Governor Andrew H. Longino. Unlike others in the group, the president, a big game hunter, had not located a bear during the hunt. His assistants cornered a black bear and tied it to a tree, inviting Roosevelt to shoot it, but he refused to do so as he saw this as unsportsmanlike. News of the incident spread across the country. A stuffed animal maker in Brooklyn, New York, created a toy bear and, after receiving permission from the president, called it "Teddy's bear."

Rowan Oak was the home of Nobel Prize winning author William Faulkner for nearly 40 years and is maintained as a museum by the university. The outline for Faulkner's Pulitzer-prize winning novel, *A Fable*, is written in graphite pencil and red grease pencil on the wall of his study.

The Square At the center of the historic square in Oxford, simply called the Square, is the Lafayette County Courthouse, built in 1874. There are various restaurants, art galleries, boutiques and shops around the Square, including Neilson's Department Store, which opened in 1839 and is the oldest department store in the South; and Square Books, an independent bookseller that has three locations on the Square. The Square is the epicenter of nightlife in town with various places where you can hear live music.

Swayze Field™ The Oxford-University Stadium is where the Ole Miss baseball team has played its home games since 1989. The stadium's playing surface was named for Tom Swayze, a former player and coach at the school.

Tad Pad™ The nickname for C.M. "Tad" Smith Coliseum,™ named in 1972 to honor the three-sport letterman, coach and university athletics director. It is where the university's men's and women's basketball teams play their home games.

Vaught Hemingway is the name of the University of Mississippi football stadium. In 1915, it was named for Judge William Hemingway, a professor of law and chairman of the university's Committee on Athletics. In 1982, the name was changed to honor Johnny Vaught also. He was the head coach of the football team from 1947 to 1970, as well as in 1973. Under Vaught, the team won six SEC Championship titles and a share of three national championships.

Ventress Hall Constructed in 1889, this building was first used as a library and now is home to the College of Liberal Arts. Inside one of the turrets, starting with a former Confederate soldier, generations of students have written their names on the wall, although this area is no longer as accessible as it once was.

Walk of Champions Before each home football game, the football team is cheered on by fans as players pass under the Walk of Champions arch and walk through the Grove on the way to Vaught-Hemingway Stadium.™ The arch was dedicated in 1998 and given to the university by the 1962 football team, winners of the SEC and national championships that year. (There was no national title game in 1962.)

Forward Rebels

Forward, Rebels, march to fame,
Hit that line and win this game!
We know that you'll fight it through,
For your colors red and blue.
Rah, rah, rah!
Rebels, you are the Southland's pride,
Take that ball and hit your stride,
Don't stop 'till the victory's won
For your Ole Miss.
Fight, fight for your Ole Miss!

The Alma Mater

Written in 1925 by W.A. Kahle and her husband, W.F. Kahle

Way down south in Mississippi,
There's a spot that ever calls.
Where among the hills enfolded,
Stand old Alma Mater's halls.
Where the trees lift high their branches,
To the whisp'ring Southern breeze.
There is Ole Miss calling, calling,
To our hearts fond memories.
With united hearts we praise thee,
All our loyalty is thine,
And we hail thee, Alma Mater,
May thy light forever shine;

May it brighter grow and brighter,
And with deep affection true,
Our thoughts shall ever cluster 'round thee,
Dear old Red and Blue.
May thy fame throughout the nation,
Through thy sons and daughters grow,
May thy name forever waken,
In our hearts a tender glow,
May thy counsel and thy spirit,
Ever keep us one in this,
That our own shall be thine honor,
Now and ever, dear Ole Miss.

About the Authors

Courtney Solon Brown graduated from the University of Mississippi with a Bachelor of Arts in Journalism and received a Master of Arts in Advertising and Public Relations from The University of Alabama. After living in Memphis and central Texas, Courtney moved to Houston where she is the owner and designer behind Mended Interiors. She and her husband welcomed the arrival of their first child, a son, in the fall of 2013. They hope their pack of dogs has helped prepare them somewhat for parenthood.

Andrea Lea graduated from the University of Mississippi with a Bachelor of Science in Chemical Engineering and received a Master of Business Administration from the University of Houston. After residing in New York City and Houston, Andi recently returned home to New Orleans where she is employed by Shell. She is enjoying the good life in her century-old Mid City home with her husband and daughter.

Ole Miss